Happy
Holi
The festival of colour

WAYLAND
www.waylandbooks.co.uk

First published in 2016 by Wayland
© Wayland 2016

Written by Joyce Bentley

Editorial consultant: Anita Ganeri
Editor: Corinne Lucas
Designer: Ariadne Ward

A catalogue for this title is
available from the British Library

ISBN: 978 0 7502 9569 7

MIX
Paper from
responsible sources
FSC® C104740

10 9 8 7 6 5 4 3 2 1

Wayland
An imprint of
Hachette Children's Books
Part of Hodder & Stoughton
Carmelite House
50 Victoria Embankment
London, EC4Y 0DZ

An Hachette UK Company
www.hachette.co.uk
www.hachettechildrens.co.uk

Printed in China

Picture credits: Cover images © Tim Gainey/Alamy Stock Photo; P4–5 ©
imageBROKER / Alamy Stock Photo; P5 © Philippe Lissac/Getty Images; P6 © ©
AnastasiaAnna/Shutterstock; P7 © © Philippe Lissac /GODONG/Getty Images; P8
© Jagdish Agarwal/Getty Images; P9 © Anil Sharma / Alamy Stock Photo; P10 ©
stockillustration/Shutterstock; P11 © Nisarg Lakhmani / Alamy Stock Photo; P12 ©
Suhaimi Abdullah / Stringer/Getty Images; P13 © Christophe Boisvieux/Getty Images;
P14 © Poras Chaudhary/Getty Images; P15 © Hindustan Times / Contributor/Alamy;
P16 © FotoFlirt / Alamy Stock Photo; P17 © Pete Niesen / Shutterstock.com; P18 ©
Hindustan Times / Contributor/Getty Images; P19 © SANJAY KANOJIA /Stringer/Getty
Images; P20–21 © Iakov Filimonov/Shutterstock; P22 © Vladyslav Starozhylov/ Alamy
Stock Photo; P23 © romawka/Shutterstock.

Background images and other graphic elements courtesy of Shutterstock.com.

Contents

What is Hinduism?

Hinduism is the oldest religion in the world and began in India over 4,000 years ago. Today, there are about one *billion* followers.

Hindus believe in a great soul or spirit, called Brahman, who is the power behind everything in the universe. Some Hindus worship Brahman as God. Hindus also worship Brahman in many different forms, through gods and goddesses.

A Hindu place of worship is known as a mandir.

Lord Krishna is a popular Hindu god.

Hindu Gods and Goddesses

In Hinduism there are many different gods and goddesses who represent Brahman's different powers. There are lots of legends about these gods and goddesses. Three of the most important gods are:

Brahma – the creator
Vishnu – the preserver
Shiva – the destroyer

The world's second largest statue of Lord Shiva, in south-east India.

The shrine is where many Hindus pray every day. Shrines contain a *murti* – an image or statue of a god or goddess – with offerings of flowers, fruit or sweets. Candles and *incense* are burnt and *sacred* words are repeated in a *mantra*.

Many Hindus have a favourite god or goddess who is special to the place they live or to their family.

Most Hindus have a shrine at home where they can worship.

7

What is Holi?

Holi is a joyful festival that celebrates the arrival of spring, in India. It was traditionally celebrated by farmers to mark the first wheat harvest of the year. Holi falls in February or March each year.

Holi is also called the 'festival of colours' because people throw coloured water and powder at each other.

There are many stories connected to Holi but the most popular ones are about the witch, Holika and the prince, Prahlad (see pages 10–11), and the god, Krishna and his wife, Radha (see pages 16–17).

Actors in Rajasthan, northern India, performing the story of Krishna and Radha.

Each region of India has its own traditions at Holi.

The Legend of Holika and Prahlad

During Holi, Hindus remember the legend of Holika and Prahlad. This story is about the victory of good over evil and the power of *devotion*.

There was once a king called Hiranyakashyap who had a son, Prahlad. The King acted like a god and demanded that everyone worship him. But his son refused, instead worshipping the god, Lord Vishnu. The King was furious with Prahlad and tried to kill him many times but each time Prahlad prayed to Lord Vishnu and was saved.

Angry with his son, the King asked his sister, Holika, to help. She had special powers that stopped her from being burnt in a fire. So she tricked Prahlad into stepping into a fire, knowing that he would die and she would survive. However, she had used her powers for evil and so she died and Prahlad lived. Hindus believe that it was Prahlad's devotion to Lord Vishnu that saved him.

Lord Vishnu

A statue of Holika, ready to be burnt on the bonfire.

Preparing for Holi

The night before Holi, Hindus remember the legend of Holika and Prahlad with a ceremony. For weeks before Holi, people collect wood, branches and twigs, and pile them up into a bonfire or *pyre*.

Women put offerings to the gods in to the pyre.

An *effigy* of Holika is placed on top of the pyre. At sunset, the fire is lit and people dance and sing around it. The effigy is burnt reminding Hindus of Holika's evil deeds.

After Holika is burnt, the sacred ashes are used to ward off evil spirits.

The Festival of Colour

On the first day of Holi, Hindus playfully throw coloured water and powder at each other, like Lord Krishna did (see page 16). Everyone is equal – old and young, rich and poor, men and women. Old clothes are worn because it is a very messy day!

People throwing coloured powder during a Holi celebration, in India.

Children love using pichkaris or water pistols to spray each other with.

Hindus gather in parks, outside of temples and by community centres to join in the festivities. Stalls selling coloured powder, jewellery, crafts and food line the streets, while people greet and wish each other 'Happy Holi'.

Traditionally, plant-based coloured powder was used but now vibrant colours are made in factories.

Krishna and Radha

Throwing coloured powder reminds Hindus of a story about Lord Krishna, one of the most popular Hindu gods. Krishna is famous for his love of mischief and playing tricks on his friends. His main companions were the beautiful Radha and her friends, the gopis (milkmaids). One day, for fun, Krishna drenched them with coloured water, and the tradition has remained.

Lord Krishna and his wife, Radha.

Krishna's playfulness is part of the Holi festival. People get together to enjoy themselves. Musicians fill the streets and there is much singing and dancing to the sounds of *dholak* (drums).

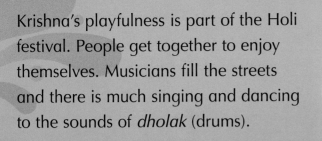

Special puppet and magic shows are put on for children, telling the story of Krishna and Radha.

An elephant festival is held during Holi in Jaipur, India, where even the animals are brightly painted.

17

A Time for Feasting

As the festivities come to an end, people go home, wash and change into their best clothes. Traditionally, people give each other sweets as gifts when they visit friends and family.

Happy and soaked in paint, these Indian girls will return home to change in to clean clothes.

Gujiyas are delicious sweet dumplings filled with dried fruit.

Thandai is popular at Holi. It is a milk-based drink made with almonds, spices and rose petals.

Food is plentiful in houses and on market stalls throughout the day. Different regions have their favourite foods but sweets and puddings are the most popular. The days before Holi are spent making sweets and delicious food such as gujiya, mathri and kachoris.

Thinking About
Holi

The Holi festival is a time for letting go
and rejoicing in life. It is about bringing
people together. Old enemies become
friends and arguments are put aside so
that everyone can celebrate as one.

Try making your own Holi word cloud. What words can you think of to describe Holi?

Holi Krishna
good evil Prahlad mathri
Radha thandai
gujiyas spring love
festival Holika powder
colour joy pichkaris
paint celebrate

Holi Greetings Card

Holi is a time when friends and family come together. But some people are unable to make the celebrations and so greetings cards are a great way of wishing them 'Happy Holi'.

Materials

Colour is the main theme of Holi so use bright, bold colours for your card. You can use coloured card, brightly coloured paints, felt-tip pens, tissue or crêpe paper to make your card. You will also need scissors, paint brushes and glue.

Your Card

To start take a piece of A4 card and fold it in half. It can be portrait or landscape. For a colourful handprint, cover the

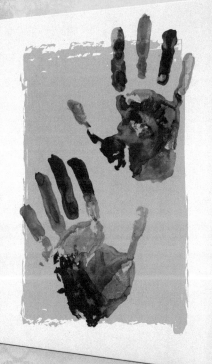

Try using some glitter paint for the handprints.

underside of your hand in different coloured paints. Then place it on the card, making sure to press your whole hand on to the card. You can make a large card with several handprints on it, or simply put one print on the card. Decorate the borders of your card with paint, felt-tip pens, tissue or crêpe paper.

Sending your card

If you are sending a card in the post you could include a small sachet of coloured powder in the envelope.

Add colourful symbols to your design or make them the main image.

Glossary

Billion – a million millions

Devotion – showing loyalty and affection to someone

Dholak – a two-headed hand drum

Effigy – a figure or image of a person

Incense – something that is burnt to make a sweet smell

Mandir – a place where Hindus worship

Mantra – repeated word or sounds used in a prayer

Murti – an image or statue of a god

Pyre – a pile of wood for burning things, such as an effigy

Pichkaris – a type of water gun

Sacred – a very important religious object

Index